I0813166

INSIDE THE NFL

CINCINNATI BENGALS

by Luke Hanlon

Abdo & Daughters
MIDDLE GRADE NONFICTION
An imprint of Abdo Publishing
abdobooks.com

ABDOBOOKS.COM

Published by Abdo Publishing, a division of ABDO, PO Box 398166, Minneapolis, Minnesota 55439.

Printed in China.
052025
092025

Cover Photos: Gregory Shamus/Getty Images Sport/Getty Images (Joe Burrow); George Gojkovich/Getty Images Sport/Getty Images (Anthony Muñoz)
Interior Photos: Andy Lyons/Getty Images Sport/Getty Images, 4–5, 8, 9, 11, 38; Dylan Buell/Getty Images Sport/Getty Images, 6, 54, 59, 61 (bottom right); Don Juan Moore/Getty Images Sport/Getty Images, 7; Abdo Publishing, 12–13; Archive Photo/Getty Images, 14–15; AP Images, 16, 18, 33, 34, 39, 60 (top), 60 (bottom right); Ron Riesterer/AP Images, 19; Tony Tomsic/AP Images, 20, 42; Clifton Boutelle/Getty Images Sport/Getty Images, 21, 26, 29; George Gelatly/Getty Images Sport/Getty Images, 22, 60 (bottom left); GS/AP Images, 23; Bettmann/Getty Images, 24–25; Brian Horton/AP Images, 27; David Durochik/AP Images, 31; Focus on Sport/Getty Images Sport/Getty Images, 32, 43; Al Messerschmidt Archive/AP Images, 35; George Gojkovich/Getty Images Sport/Getty Images, 36–37; Jonathan Daniel/Getty Images Sport/Getty Images, 40; Rick Stewart/Getty Images Sport/Getty Images, 41; Rob Brown/Getty Images Sport/Getty Images, 44, 63; Kathy Willens/AP Images, 45; Mitchell Layton/Getty Images Sport/Getty Images, 46–47; Al Behrman/AP Images, 48; G. Newman Lowrance/AP Images, 49; Logan Bowles/AP Images, 50, 61 (top); Tony Tribble/AP Images, 51; Michael Owens/Getty Images Sport/Getty Images, 52, 61 (bottom left); Jamie Squire/Getty Images Sport/Getty Images, 55, 56; Steph Chambers/Getty Images Sport/Getty Images, 57; Shutterstock Images, 58

Editor: Chrös McDougall
Series Designer: Laura Graphenteen
Production Designer: Ryan Gale

Library of Congress Control Number: 2024948490

Publisher's Cataloging-in-Publication Data

Names: Hanlon, Luke, author.
Title: Cincinnati Bengals / by Luke Hanlon
Description: Minneapolis, Minnesota: Abdo Publishing, 2026 | Series: Inside the NFL | Includes online resources and index.
Identifiers: ISBN 9781098296681 (lib. bdg.) | ISBN 9798384919209 (ebook)
Subjects: LCSH: Cincinnati Bengals (Football team)--Juvenile literature. | National Football League--Juvenile literature. | Football teams--Juvenile literature. | American football--Juvenile literature.
Classification: DDC 796.333--dc23

CONTENTS

Bengals quarterback Joe Burrow passed for 4,611 yards in 2021.

CHAPTER 1

CAN'T STOP CHASE

Joe Burrow dropped back to pass. The Cincinnati Bengals quarterback had a target in mind. Throughout the 2021 National Football League (NFL) season, he and rookie wide receiver Ja'Marr Chase seemed to have a special connection. Now, in Week 17, they needed to show it again.

Behind the two stars, Cincinnati was a team on the rise. A win would clinch the Bengals' first division title in six years. But the opposing Kansas City Chiefs had played in the previous two Super Bowls. That established them as the clear team to beat in the American Football Conference (AFC). And now the Chiefs led 14–0 in the second-to-last game of the season.

Chase ran to an open space on the left side of the field. He turned just in time for Burrow to zip a pass his way. Immediately, four Chiefs defenders

Ja'Marr Chase (1) breaks away from the Kansas City defense during their Week 17 game in 2021.

closed in. Spinning around, Chase juked past one defender and cut upfield. Eight Chiefs raced after him. They had no chance. Chase blew past the pack and sprinted for a 72-yard touchdown. Just like that, the Chiefs' lead was down to seven. But the Bengals still had a long way to go.

REUNITING CHAMPIONS

The Bengals had experienced both very good and very bad seasons in their history. They had reached the Super Bowl twice during the 1980s. But in 2019, Cincinnati was in a bad way. With a 2–14 record, the Bengals were the league's worst team. There was reason for fans to be optimistic, though. All those losses led to the Bengals getting the top pick in the 2020 NFL Draft. Cincinnati used that pick on Burrow, a strong-armed passer who had just led Louisiana State University (LSU) to the college national championship.

With Burrow under center in 2020, the Bengals did a little better. They still went into the 2021 draft with the fifth overall pick. The Bengals wanted to get Burrow another weapon on offense. And they had just the player in mind. Burrow and Chase had made a dynamic combination during their time at LSU together. As a sophomore in 2019, Chase led the Tigers in receiving yards and touchdowns. And when the receiver was still on the board in the 2021 draft, the Bengals grabbed him.

The pair quickly picked up where they'd left off. In Chase's NFL debut, he caught five passes for 101 yards and a touchdown in a win against the Minnesota Vikings. Games like that soon became routine. Heading into the Week 17 matchup against the Chiefs,

READY FOR THE BRIGHT LIGHTS

Joe Burrow and Ja'Marr Chase played at their best when it mattered most for LSU in 2019. That season, LSU faced Clemson in the national championship game. Clemson had no answers for LSU's explosive offense. Burrow threw for 463 yards and five touchdowns while running for a sixth. Chase caught two touchdowns from Burrow and set a championship game record with 221 receiving yards. Meanwhile, Burrow's 521 total yards of offense set a record as well.

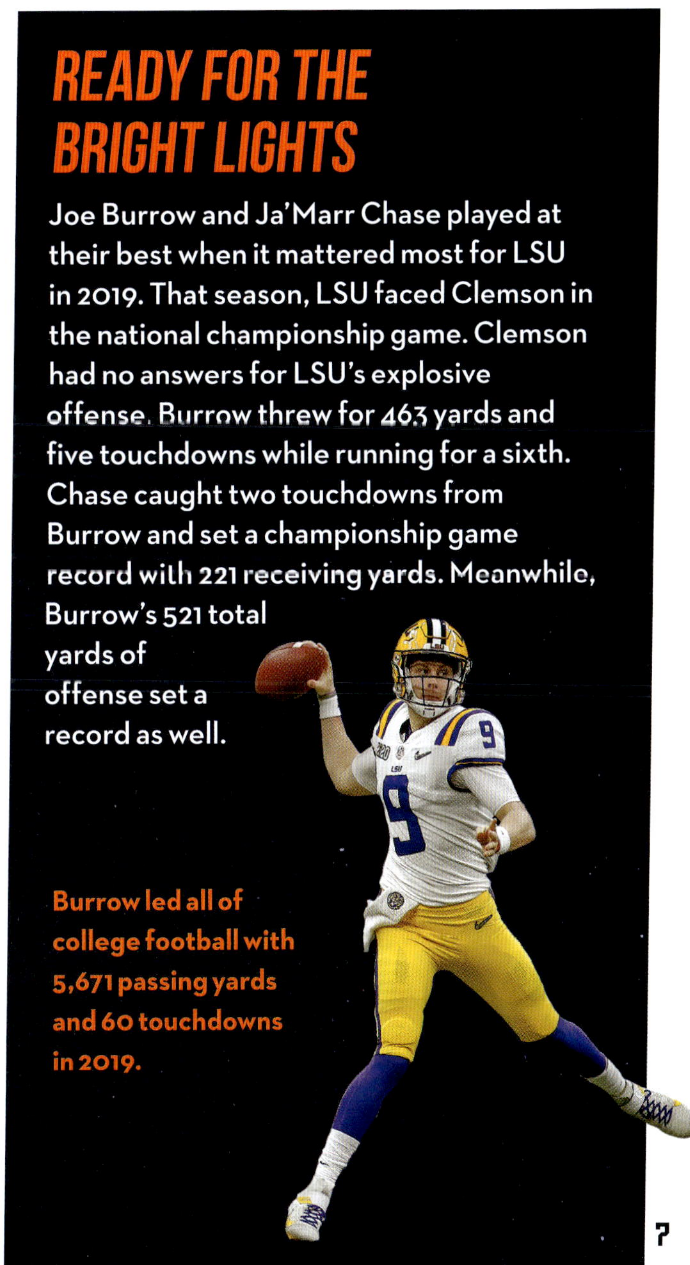

Burrow led all of college football with 5,671 passing yards and 60 touchdowns in 2019.

the rookie had already racked up 1,163 yards and 10 touchdowns. More importantly, Burrow and Chase had led the Bengals to a 9–6 record and the cusp of a division title. They just had to beat the Chiefs.

UNSTOPPABLE

Chase's long touchdown brought the Bengals to within seven points. However, the Chiefs quickly reminded fans how dominant their offense could be. They completed a long touchdown drive to go up 21–7. If the Bengals were going to win, they'd have to do it in a shootout. And so that's what they set out to do.

Chase hangs on to a touchdown catch against the Chiefs.

Eight plays into their next drive, the Bengals faced first-and-10 from the Kansas City 18-yard line. Chase, with a Chiefs cornerback shadowing him, ran straight up the right sideline. Burrow lofted a pass his way anyway. Shaking off his defender, the 6-foot, 201-pound Chase leaped into the air and grabbed the ball. Then he carefully tapped both feet in the end zone for another score. That brought Cincinnati to within seven points. However, by halftime the Chiefs extended their lead to 28–17.

The Bengals were going to need a huge second half to come back against the Chiefs. That began three plays in when Chase took off on a go route down the left sideline. Seeing the open receiver, Burrow quickly threw a pass his way. Catching it in stride, Chase ran untouched for a 69-yard touchdown. The score cut Kansas City's lead to four points. Then Burrow threw another touchdown, this one to wide receiver Tyler Boyd, to put his team up 31–28 early in the fourth quarter. Once again, though, the Chiefs quickly answered. This time, they made a field goal to tie the game 31–31.

The teams remained deadlocked when the Bengals got the ball back with 6:01 to play. Cincinnati began at its own 25-yard line. Facing an aggressive Chiefs defense, Burrow

Burrow threw for 446 yards in the Week 17 game against the Chiefs.

remained in command. On the fourth play, he hit Chase, who escaped tight coverage to secure a 35-yard gain. Three plays later, on third-and-27, Burrow shook off the blitzing Chiefs and launched another pass to Chase. Chase caught the ball over a defender for a 30-yard gain and a clutch first down. Three plays after that, the Bengals reached the 2-yard line.

With 2:10 remaining, Cincinnati just needed to run out the clock and kick an easy field goal to pull off the victory and claim a division title. The Chiefs weren't about to give up, though. A fierce goal-line stand soon put the Bengals at fourth down and just inches from the end zone. Now they had a big decision to make. Fifty-seven seconds remained on the clock. While a field goal would put the Bengals up, it would also mean giving the ball back to the Chiefs with nearly a minute to play.

"I knew we'd go for it," Burrow said. "They've got Patrick Mahomes on the other side. He could go down and win the game."

"I KNEW WE'D GO FOR IT. THEY'VE GOT PATRICK MAHOMES ON THE OTHER SIDE. HE COULD GO DOWN AND WIN THE GAME."

—JOE BURROW

Burrow and the offense indeed stayed on the field, hoping to get the first down and run off more time. Instead, Burrow threw an incomplete pass to turn the ball over on downs. The Bengals got a huge break, however. Kansas City was called for a penalty, giving Cincinnati a new set of downs. The Bengals burned two of them to run the clock down to two seconds. Finally, as time expired, kicker Evan McPherson drilled a 20-yard field goal. After several difficult seasons, the Bengals secured a 34–31 win and once again showed they could be among the NFL's very best.

Evan McPherson blasts a kick against the Chiefs in Week 17 of the 2021 season.

NFL TEAMS MAP

NFC

NFC EAST

DALLAS COWBOYS

NEW YORK GIANTS

PHILADELPHIA EAGLES

WASHINGTON COMMANDERS

NFC WEST

ARIZONA CARDINALS

LOS ANGELES RAMS

SAN FRANCISCO 49ERS

SEATTLE SEAHAWKS

NFC NORTH

CHICAGO BEARS

DETROIT LIONS

GREEN BAY PACKERS

MINNESOTA VIKINGS

NFC SOUTH

ATLANTA FALCONS

CAROLINA PANTHERS

NEW ORLEANS SAINTS

TAMPA BAY BUCCANEERS

AFC

AFC EAST

- BUFFALO BILLS
- MIAMI DOLPHINS

- NEW ENGLAND PATRIOTS
- NEW YORK JETS

AFC WEST

- DENVER BRONCOS
- KANSAS CITY CHIEFS

- LAS VEGAS RAIDERS
- LOS ANGELES CHARGERS

AFC NORTH

- BALTIMORE RAVENS
- CINCINNATI BENGALS

- CLEVELAND BROWNS
- PITTSBURGH STEELERS

AFC SOUTH

- HOUSTON TEXANS
- INDIANAPOLIS COLTS

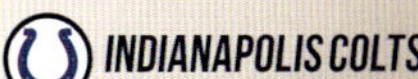

- JACKSONVILLE JAGUARS

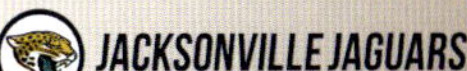

- TENNESSEE TITANS

Paul Brown was 37 when he started coaching the Cleveland Browns.

CHAPTER 2

OHIO ORIGINS

The Cleveland Browns had been named for Paul Brown. And during his 17 years as Cleveland's coach and general manager, Brown led his namesake team to seven championships. So when team owner Art Modell controversially fired Brown in 1963, fans were more than stunned. They were angry. Even NFL commissioner Pete Rozelle tried to convince Modell to reverse course. But there was no changing Modell's mind.

Brown had an unmatched résumé at the time. His teams had won at every level. He'd also revolutionized the game, especially during his time with the Browns. Among his innovations were hiring the NFL's first full-time coaching staff, calling plays from the sideline, and introducing film study. In 1946, he helped break the sport's color barrier when he signed two Black players.

And using his inventive schemes on the field, the Browns won a lot. Many credit Brown with helping to usher football into the big-time sport it is today.

"Whether they know it or not, nearly everyone in the game of football has been affected by Paul Brown," Rozelle said. "His wealth of ideas changed the game."

"WHETHER THEY KNOW IT OR NOT, NEARLY EVERYONE IN THE GAME OF FOOTBALL HAS BEEN AFFECTED BY PAUL BROWN. HIS WEALTH OF IDEAS CHANGED THE GAME."

—PETE ROZELLE

It was little surprise that other teams were interested in hiring Brown. And at 54, Brown was eager to keep coaching. However, no teams were offering Brown an opportunity to both coach and control the roster. Instead, Brown began looking into starting his own team.

Brown's innovations as a football coach still impact the game today.

BORN IN OHIO

When deciding on his next steps, Brown naturally looked to Ohio. He had been born in Norwalk, in the northern part of the state. After playing quarterback for Miami University in southwestern Ohio, he later became the coach at his alma mater, Massillon High School. Over nine seasons there, Brown led Massillon to six straight Ohio state championships. Then he moved on to Ohio State, where he led the Buckeyes to their first national title in 1942. That led to his time in Cleveland with the Browns. So, when looking for his next opportunity, Brown wasn't looking to go too far.

In 1965, Brown met with Jim Rhodes, the governor of Ohio, to discuss the possibility of bringing another pro football team to the state. With Rhodes's support, Brown considered Columbus and Cincinnati as two possible homes. When Cincinnati offered to build a new multiuse stadium for Major League Baseball's Cincinnati Reds to share with a new football team, the choice became clear. However, Brown still needed a team.

HISTORIC NAME

When deciding on a name for his new team, Paul Brown looked to honor the city's football history. A different team called the Bengals had played in Cincinnati during the late 1930s and early 1940s. It was named for a white Bengal tiger on display at the Cincinnati Zoo. Cincinnati had also been home to early pro football teams called the Celts and the Reds.

The 1960s were a time of disruption in pro football. Many cities wanted to join the NFL. When the league declined to add new teams, the American Football League (AFL) was founded in 1960 as an alternative. Though many initially looked down on the AFL, the

Brown examines different helmet options for the Bengals ahead of their 1968 debut.

upstart league quickly showed it was for real. By the 1966 season, the NFL and AFL announced they would merge and become a single league by 1970.

Brown's focus had been on rejoining the NFL. As it turned out, the AFL provided an opportunity to get there. The league had nine teams and sought a 10th before the merger. In 1967, the AFL announced Cincinnati would be that 10th team, with Brown acting as the owner, general manager, and head coach. It proved to be a savvy move for both sides. Brown got a chance to own a team that would soon be in the NFL. Meanwhile, having Brown, who entered the Pro Football Hall of Fame in 1967, helped build up the AFL's credibility ahead of the merger.

TAKING THE FIELD

Few knew what to expect once the Bengals took the field for the first time on September 6, 1968. As an expansion team, they had a roster made up mostly of castoffs from other AFL teams. And that showed in a lopsided loss in the team's debut against the Chargers in San Diego. But Cincinnati came home the next week to beat the Denver Broncos 24–10. Then the Bengals beat the Buffalo Bills, too. After that, however, the season imploded as the team lost 10 of its final 11 games.

Bengals lineman Harry Gunner, *right*, chases down Oakland Raiders quarterback Daryle Lamonica during an October 1968 game.

Quarterback Sam Wyche, *right*, played 24 games for the Bengals from 1968 to 1970.

Even with the rough start, the team showed some promise. Tight end Bob Trumpy, who the team found in the 12th round of that year's draft, caught four passes for 114 yards and a touchdown in the win against Denver. He became one of three Bengals rookies to make the AFL All-Star Game, along with center Bob Johnson and running back Paul Robinson. Robinson also earned AFL Rookie of the Year honors after leading the league in rushing.

Brown showcased his strong scouting ability again in the 1969 draft when he took Ken Riley in the sixth round. Despite playing quarterback in college, Riley became a cornerback for the Bengals and recorded four interceptions as a rookie. He was a key part of Cincinnati's defense for years to come.

Big changes arrived in 1970. After playing their first two seasons at the University of Cincinnati's stadium, the Bengals moved into the new Riverfront Stadium, a multipurpose venue located along

Cornerback Ken Riley intercepted a Bengals-record 65 passes between 1969 and 1983.

Wyche, *center*, hands the ball to running back Jess Phillips during a 1970 game against the Detroit Lions.

the Ohio River in downtown Cincinnati. That year also marked the completion of the AFL-NFL merger. As part of the change, three NFL teams joined the 10 AFL teams to make up the AFC. Among the teams to make the switch was the Browns. That meant the Ohio rivals would play twice every season.

The Browns beat the Bengals 30–27 in the first "Battle of Ohio," which took place in Week 4 of the 1970 season. The loss was part of a 1–6 start for the Bengals. Five weeks later, the Browns showed up at Riverfront Stadium and quickly jumped out to a 10–0 lead. This time, though, the Bengals roared back. Fullback Jess Phillips caught a touchdown pass, and then Robinson charged into the end zone for another. That was enough to give the Bengals a 14–10 win, sending the more than 60,000 Cincinnati fans home happy.

From there, the Bengals pulled off a seven-game win streak to finish the season 8–6. That record was good enough to finish one game ahead of the Browns to win the AFC Central Division title. Brown won the NFL Coach of the Year Award as the Bengals became the quickest expansion team to ever make the playoffs. The Baltimore Colts proved to be too much to handle in the postseason, beating the Bengals 17–0. But Brown and his Bengals appeared to be heading in the right direction.

Bengals running back Paul Robinson (18) dives into the end zone for a score in Cincinnati's 14–10 win over the Cleveland Browns in 1970.

Bengals quarterback Ken Anderson started four games as a rookie in 1971.

CHAPTER 3

A NEW LEADER

The Bengals decided to shake up their quarterback room ahead of the 1971 season. Virgil Carter had been the primary starter throughout the 1970 season and led the team to the playoffs. So, the Bengals felt comfortable to trade away backup quarterback Sam Wyche during the offseason. Then, in the 1971 draft, the Bengals selected quarterback Ken Anderson to sit and learn behind Carter.

Those plans changed when Carter suffered an injury in Week 3, forcing Anderson into action. Anderson didn't win any of his four starts in 1971, but he showed promise as the Bengals finished 4–10. After splitting time with Carter as a rookie, Anderson became the starter in 1972. In an era when even the best quarterbacks struggled to complete half their passes, he proved to be incredibly accurate. Over 16 years under center for the Bengals, Anderson set several passing records that still stood 30 years after he left the team.

Even with their sharpshooting quarterback, the Bengals offense was powered by its two running backs in 1973. Veteran Essex Johnson piled up 997 yards that season. Hulking rookie Boobie Clark, a 12th-round pick, ran for 988. The dynamic backfield duo helped the Bengals win 10 games and clinch the AFC Central title. The running game came undone in the playoffs, however. Neither back could get anything going against the Miami Dolphins. The defending Super Bowl champions stomped the Bengals 34–16.

Running back Essex Johnson ran for more than 500 yards in three different seasons with the Bengals.

A LEGEND LEAVES THE SIDELINE

Bill Walsh is one of the NFL's most successful coaches. Running his signature West Coast offense, his San Francisco 49ers won three

Bill Walsh, *left*, developed his famous offensive scheme during his time as an assistant coach with the Bengals.

Super Bowls in the 1980s. A decade earlier, Walsh was establishing that scheme in Cincinnati.

Paul Brown hired Walsh as a promising young assistant coach for his original Bengals coaching staff in 1968. By 1971, Walsh was coaching the team's quarterbacks and calling plays on offense. Before long, Cincinnati was thriving with the familiar pattern of short passes that San Francisco would later make famous.

"TO CALL IT THE WEST COAST OFFENSE IS ALMOST FUNNY, BECAUSE THE PLAYS WERE THE SAME [THAT WE RAN IN CINCINNATI]. THE 'MIDWEST OFFENSE' MIGHT BE A BETTER MONIKER FOR IT."

—DAVE LAPHAM

"To call it the West Coast offense is almost funny, because the plays were the same [that we ran in Cincinnati]," said Dave Lapham, a Bengals offensive lineman. "The 'Midwest offense' might be a better moniker for it."

Though the offense didn't always lead to wins early on, Anderson grew more and more comfortable leading it. In 1973, he led the Bengals to 10 wins and a return to the playoffs. Two years later, he threw for an NFL-leading 3,169 yards as the Bengals won a team-record 11 games. Now fans wanted to see the team bring that success to the playoffs.

The Oakland Raiders had other ideas. Playing at home, they built a 24–7 lead early in the second half. Finally, the Bengals offense woke up. The teams traded touchdowns, and then defensive back Ken Riley grabbed an interception to get the ball back for Cincinnati. Two plays later, Anderson found wide receiver Charlie Joiner for a 25-yard touchdown. The quarterback then hit Pro Bowl wide receiver Isaac Curtis for a leaping touchdown on the next possession to pull within three points. When Cincinnati recovered a fumble to regain possession, the improbable comeback appeared within reach. However, those hopes died when Oakland's defense stepped up to secure a 31–28 win.

After their slow start, the Bengals had become a competitive team. In the six years from 1970 to 1975, the team posted just one losing season. It reached the playoffs three times. Each time, however, ended with a first-round loss. The playoff struggles deeply

Bengals wide receiver Isaac Curtis made the Pro Bowl in his first four seasons.

upset Brown. Four days after losing to the Raiders, he let the team know that he would be stepping down as head coach. Remaining the team's owner and general manager, he named offensive line coach Tiger Johnson as the team's new head coach. This news shocked Walsh, who thought he had done enough to earn the head coaching job. Instead of sticking around in Cincinnati, Walsh left the Bengals to go work for the San Diego Chargers.

BEEFING UP

The Bengals began to decline without Brown coaching them. Johnson was fired after starting 0–5 in 1978. His replacement, Homer Rice, didn't do much better. The 1979 season marked the

Bengals' fourth in a row without making the playoffs. So, Brown decided to make another change and hired Forrest Gregg. He had been a Hall of Fame offensive lineman for the Green Bay Packers. Brown hoped his toughness as a player would translate to the players he coached.

For Gregg, that process started in the 1980 draft. The Bengals held the third pick. Gregg wanted to use it on the best offensive lineman he could find. On one scouting trip, he traveled to the University of Southern California (USC). Anthony Muñoz appeared to have all the tools of a great lineman, though he had struggled with injuries in college. Gregg wanted to see the super athletic big man in person.

Near the end of the workout, Gregg ran a one-on-one drill in which he acted like a defensive lineman trying to get past Muñoz. The 6-foot-6, 278-pound Muñoz drove both of his hands into Gregg's chest and knocked him to the ground. Muñoz apologized, thinking he had blown his chance to play for the Bengals. Gregg simply smiled, impressed by Muñoz's strength. "When he did that, I said, 'We've got to have this guy,'" Gregg said. The Bengals selected Muñoz with the third pick, and he became the team's starting left tackle as a rookie.

EARN YOUR STRIPES

Starting in the team's first season in 1968, Cincinnati wore all-orange helmets with "Bengals" written in black lettering. In 1981, the team removed the letters and replaced them with six black tiger stripes that ran from one side of the helmet to the other. Paul Brown made the change to help differentiate Cincinnati's helmets from the Cleveland Browns' all-orange helmets. The new design proved popular among fans, and the Bengals have worn it ever since.

Offensive tackle Anthony Muñoz made 11 Pro Bowls with the Bengals.

QUICK TURNAROUND

Anderson missed three games in 1980, and the Bengals finished Gregg's first season 6–10. Then the team got off to a disastrous start in 1981. Hosting the Seattle Seahawks in Week 1, the Bengals fell behind 21–0 in the first quarter. Needing to change something, Gregg benched Anderson and brought in backup Turk Schonert. The move worked. Behind Schonert, the Bengals scored 27 unanswered points to start the season with a win.

Despite Schonert's heroics, Gregg stuck with the veteran Anderson as his starter. That decision paid off, as Anderson had the best season of his career. A big reason for that was the addition of rookie wide receiver Cris Collinsworth, who quickly became a go-to target for Anderson. With the fast and lanky Collinsworth to throw to and the powerful Muñoz blocking for him, Anderson passed for a career-high 3,754 yards and 29 touchdowns. His play helped the Bengals to a 12–4 record while earning him the NFL's Most Valuable Player (MVP) Award.

Wide receiver Cris Collinsworth made the Pro Bowl in his first three seasons with the Bengals.

With the AFC's best record, the Bengals hosted the Buffalo Bills in the divisional round of the playoffs. It quickly turned into a back-and-forth battle. Buffalo scored early in the fourth quarter to tie the game 21–21. On the next drive, Anderson marched the Bengals into the red zone. A quick throw found Collinsworth alone

The Bengals line up against the San Diego Chargers during the AFC title game on January 10, 1982.

in the middle of the field. He walked into the end zone untouched to put the Bengals up 28–21. Cincinnati's defense did the rest, giving the Bengals their first playoff win in team history.

Next up were the San Diego Chargers. They arrived at Cincinnati's Riverfront Stadium for the AFC Championship Game to find biting winter weather. The temperature was –9 degrees Fahrenheit (–22°C) at kickoff. Gusting winds made it feel as cold as –59 degrees Fahrenheit (–51°C). Trying to intimidate their opponents from sunny Southern California, the Bengals' offensive

The Bengals carry coach Forrest Gregg off the field after winning the AFC Championship Game on January 8, 1989. The victory sent them on to Super Bowl XVI.

and defensive linemen went without long sleeves. The Chargers struggled to handle the freezing temperatures and turned the ball over four times. With a 27–7 victory, the Bengals earned a trip to Super Bowl XVI.

A familiar face awaited the Bengals. Bill Walsh had taken over as the San Francisco 49ers head coach in 1979. Using his West Coast offense, he quickly turned the team into a National Football Conference (NFC) power. That offense was on full display in the first half of the Super Bowl. San Francisco quarterback Joe Montana ran and threw for a touchdown as the 49ers jumped out to a 20–0 lead.

Anderson finally began to play like the MVP in the second half. He ran for a touchdown in the third quarter to put the Bengals on the board. Later in the third quarter, Anderson drove the Bengals to San Francisco's 1-yard line. The Bengals ran three different plays near the goal line, looking to reduce the deficit to six points. However, the 49ers defense wouldn't budge and blew up each play at the line of scrimmage. The 49ers carried the momentum of that goal-line stand for the rest of the game and held on for a 26–21 win. Six years after the Bengals decided not to hire Walsh, he ended their Super Bowl dreams.

San Francisco defenders stuff Cincinnati fullback Pete Johnson (46) at the goal line during Super Bowl XVI.

The Bengals' Anthony Muñoz prepares to block a Houston Oilers defender in a 1982 game.

CHAPTER 4

AN UNEXPECTED CHANGE

THE BENGALS HAD ACHIEVED AN INCREDIBLE TURNAROUND IN COACH Forrest Gregg's first two seasons. Then they got off to a promising start in 1982, winning their opener before falling in overtime in Week 2. However, a players' strike shut down the league after that.

The players eventually returned in November, and the Bengals got right back to work. With time to play only seven more regular-season games, the Bengals won six of them to finish 7–2. Behind star players such as Ken Anderson, Cris Collinsworth, Anthony Muñoz, and Ken Riley, Cincinnati entered the playoffs with momentum.

Bengals fans were dreaming of another Super Bowl run when their team jumped out to an early 14–3 lead over the New York Jets in the playoff opener. That proved to be the high point.

Everything soon fell apart as the Jets rallied to win 44–17 in front of a stunned crowd at Riverfront Stadium.

Though the Bengals took a step back in 1983, going 7–9, Gregg still had a year left on his contract, and Paul Brown had no plans to end it early. However, when the Green Bay Packers' head coaching job came open, Gregg expressed interest in it. Brown knew Gregg had a strong connection with his former team, so he let him go. Just like that, the only coach to win a playoff game in team history was gone.

A NEW NO-HUDDLE ERA

Brown looked to one of his former players, Sam Wyche, to replace Gregg. Wyche had been a backup quarterback for the Bengals from 1968 to 1970. He started his coaching career as the San Francisco 49ers quarterbacks coach, helping Joe Montana become a superstar.

Like Brown and Bill Walsh before him, Wyche developed an innovative new offense in Cincinnati. His no-huddle offense was designed to run plays quickly to tire out the opposing defense. And he had a player in mind to eventually run it. The Bengals selected

WHO DEY

Whenever the Bengals score a touchdown during a home game, the fans in Cincinnati celebrate with the same chant. They all yell, "Who dey? Who dey? Who dey think gonna beat dem Bengals? Nobody!" There are disputes over the origin of the chant. But it first became popular during the team's run to the Super Bowl in the 1981 season. Since then, it's become a beloved tradition in Cincinnati.

Boomer Esiason was the first quarterback taken in the 1984 draft.

quarterback Boomer Esiason in the second round of the 1984 draft. Within a year, the lefty quarterback had replaced the aging Anderson. Esiason played at a high level in Wyche's system. But that didn't always lead to wins.

MOVING FAST

While Esiason and the Bengals showed some promise, they hadn't been able to put everything together. Many fans and media members thought Wyche would be fired after a disappointing 1987 season. However, he still had one more year on his contract. Brown, convinced that the bad season was a fluke due to another players' strike, decided to stick with the coach. His patience paid off in a big way. By the 1988 season, Esiason had mastered the no-huddle offense and tormented defenses with it.

On top of their high-powered passing game, the Bengals could also gash opponents on the ground with their two standout running

Bengals running back James Brooks ran for 931 yards and eight touchdowns in 1988.

backs, Ickey Woods and James Brooks. With talent all over the field, the Bengals led the NFL in scoring while racing to a 12–4 record. Esiason was named the league's MVP.

In the playoffs, opponents did all they could to stop the no-huddle offense. Throughout a divisional round game against Seattle, Seahawks defenders faked injuries and stayed down on the field to give their defense a rest. While the strategy slowed down Cincinnati's passing attack, the Bengals still ran all over the Seahawks. Behind 254 rushing yards, the Bengals raced to a 21–0 lead at halftime before winning 21–13.

That set up an AFC Championship Game showdown against the Buffalo Bills. Ahead of the game, Bills coach Marv Levy encouraged the league commissioner to ban the no-huddle offense. Two hours before kickoff, the league announced that the ball could not be snapped quickly prior to the final two minutes of either half, and neither team could fake injuries.

Wyche was furious. The offensive strategy the Bengals had used all season would now be restricted in the biggest game of their season. But the Bengals players weren't worried. They hadn't lost a home game all season, including against the Bills in Week 13.

"WE KNEW WE WERE GOING TO BEAT THEM AGAIN, ESPECIALLY AT HOME. NOBODY CAME INTO 'THE JUNGLE' AND BEAT US THERE. WE'D ALREADY KNEW WE WERE GOING TO BEAT THE BILLS."

—ICKEY WOODS

"We knew we were going to beat them again, especially at home," Woods said later. "Nobody came into 'The Jungle' and beat us there. We'd already knew we were going to beat the Bills."

Woods backed that up on the field. Running behind Muñoz and a stacked offensive line, the rookie ran for the opening score in the first quarter and then extended the Bengals' lead in the fourth. Each time, he celebrated by running to the sidelines and doing "the Ickey Shuffle," his signature touchdown dance. He'd take two steps to the right, two to the left, and then another two to the right before spiking the ball. Woods ended the

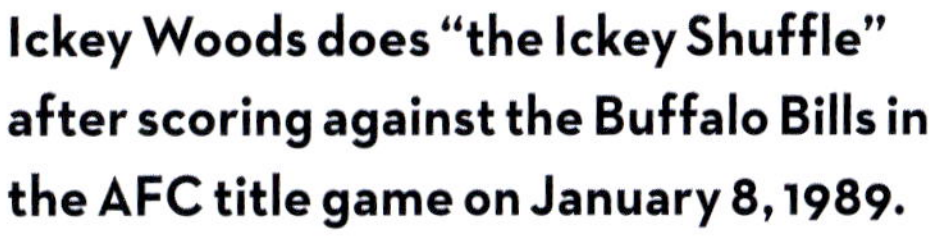

Ickey Woods does "the Ickey Shuffle" after scoring against the Buffalo Bills in the AFC title game on January 8, 1989.

Bengals defensive tackle Tim Krumrie takes down a San Francisco 49ers running back during Super Bowl XXIII on January 22, 1989.

game with 102 rushing yards as the Bengals danced their way to Super Bowl XXIII with a 21–10 win.

FAMILIAR FOE

In a rematch of Super Bowl XVI seven years earlier, the Bengals again faced the San Francisco 49ers in Super Bowl XXIII. While Cincinnati had a new coach and quarterback leading the way, Bill Walsh and Joe Montana had the 49ers on the brink of a dynasty. They had added a second championship following the 1984 season and appeared on their way to becoming the league's dominant team of the 1980s.

While both teams were best known for their offenses, each had key stars on defense, too. Pro Bowl defensive tackle Tim Krumrie led the way for Cincinnati. The bruising lineman often stuffed plays behind the line of scrimmage. And he racked up tackles like he was a linebacker. Throughout his career, Krumrie was known for his durability and toughness. But in the first quarter of the Super Bowl, Krumrie tried to make a tackle and broke his leg. It seemed as if Montana and the high-powered 49ers offense would feast on the Bengals with Krumrie out. Yet, the Bengals' defense held strong, and they led San Francisco 6–3 midway through the third quarter.

The 49ers tied the game with a field goal later in the quarter. On the ensuing kickoff, Stanford Jennings caught the ball at his own 7-yard line. Five blockers set up right in front of him. They cleared a path down the middle of the field, and Jennings burst right down it. He returned the kickoff 93 yards for the game's first touchdown.

However, Montana and the 49ers quickly answered. On the next possession, the quarterback homed in on his superstar wide receiver Jerry Rice. The duo connected for a 31-yard gain to start the drive. Then they ended it with a 14-yard score to tie the game 13–13.

After a stalled drive from each team, Esiason and the Bengals got the ball back with 8:47 to go. The quarterback led a 10-play

The 49ers' Charles Haley hits Esiason during Super Bowl XXIII.

Running back Stanford Jennings breaks away from San Francisco defenders during Super Bowl XXIII.

drive that lasted more than five minutes and ended with a field goal to put the Bengals up 16–13. The 49ers got the ball back on their own 8-yard line with 3:20 to go.

Known as "Joe Cool," Montana again appeared unfazed by the pressure. He completed seven passes to bring the 49ers down to Cincinnati's 10-yard line. He then threaded a pass between two defenders to connect with wide receiver John Taylor for the game-winning touchdown with 34 seconds left. Just like they did seven years prior, Montana and Walsh spoiled Cincinnati's hopes of becoming Super Bowl champions.

Bengals kicker Jim Breech, *left*, and wide receiver Cris Collinsworth watch the clock wind down at the end of Super Bowl XXIII.

Sam Wyche went 61–66 in eight seasons as Cincinnati's coach.

CHAPTER 5

ENDING THE DROUGHT

The Bengals went from being nine yards shy of a Super Bowl win in the 1988 season to an 8–8 record and missing the playoffs altogether in 1989. Though they recovered to make the playoffs again in 1990, the team's fortunes soon crumbled. It began when Paul Brown died at the age of 82 prior to the 1991 season. Though he hadn't coached the team since 1975, Brown still ran its operations. He was a giant in the football world.

Paul Brown's son, Mike Brown, took over as the team's owner. He had been working for the team since its founding in 1968. But his ownership got off to a rocky start. After a 3–13 record in 1991, Brown held a meeting with Sam Wyche. Brown said the coach resigned in that meeting, while Wyche told reporters that Brown fired him. Either way, Wyche was gone. And without his trusted coach, Boomer Esiason didn't want to stick around either. He demanded a trade and was gone by 1993.

That set the stage for a miserable decade in Cincinnati. While cycling through four different coaches, the team failed to produce a winning record in each of the 13 seasons after Wyche left. Some seasons got so bad that fans began referring to the team as "the Bungles."

FINDING CONSISTENCY

When looking for a new coach to take over before the 2003 season, Mike Brown tried something different. Every Bengals head coach since Forrest Gregg had some previous experience with the team. So instead, Brown looked outward in hiring Marvin Lewis. As defensive coordinator for the Baltimore Ravens, Lewis had guided one of the league's all-time dominant defenses in 2000, which led the team to its first Super Bowl title. Brown hoped Lewis could establish a similar bruising defense in Cincinnati.

The Bengals made another key addition before the 2003 season. In that year's draft, they used the first overall pick to take quarterback Carson Palmer. The USC star was coming off a Heisman Trophy as college football's best player in 2002.

Marvin Lewis had established himself as a great defensive coordinator before becoming head coach of the Bengals.

After finishing a franchise worst 2–14 in 2002, the Bengals improved to 8–8 the next two seasons. Palmer showed promise in his first year as a starter in 2004. In 2005, running back Rudi Johnson ran for 1,458 yards while Palmer threw a league-high 32 touchdowns. Half of them went to star receivers Chad Johnson and T. J. Houshmandzadeh. Behind this explosive offense, the Bengals won 11 games to earn the division title and post the team's first winning record since 1990.

The playoffs couldn't have started worse, however. On the second offensive play of the opener, a Pittsburgh Steelers defender dived into Palmer's knee. With an injured Palmer watching from the sideline, the Steelers went on to win 31–17.

An injury to quarterback Carson Palmer ended the Bengals' 2005 season on a sour note.

Behind Palmer, Johnson, and Houshmandzadeh, the Bengals remained an exciting and explosive team. However, they made the playoffs just once in the next five seasons, falling at home to the New York Jets in the 2009 wild-card round. Following a disappointing 4–12 season in 2010, Palmer demanded a trade. Instead, Brown refused to trade him away and set his sights on finding a replacement in the draft.

EARLY EXITS

The Bengals waited until the second round of the 2011 draft to select quarterback Andy Dalton. By then, they'd already picked up a key weapon for him to throw to. Wide receiver A. J. Green arrived in Cincinnati with the fourth overall pick.

A. J. Green, *right*, proved to be one of the NFL's most dangerous wide receivers during his time with the Bengals from 2011 to 2020.

Dalton earned the starting job right away, and he played well enough as a rookie that Brown finally agreed to trade Palmer midway through the 2011 season. It helped Dalton that Green got off to a fast start too, racking up more than 1,000 receiving yards. Behind the two Pro Bowl rookies, the Bengals won nine games and returned to the playoffs. However, Dalton threw three interceptions in a 31–10 loss to the Houston Texans.

Dalton and Green kept the Bengals competitive for years. Meanwhile, Lewis consistently put together stingy defenses led by star defensive tackle Geno Atkins. Starting with the 2011 season, the Bengals made the playoffs four years in a row. However, the team lost in the wild-card round each time, with Dalton throwing six interceptions and one touchdown in the four games.

Finally, the 2015 season appeared to be different. Dalton and Green tore up defenses as Cincinnati started 8–0. The Bengals finished with a 12–4 record to win the competitive AFC North. But a late-season thumb injury sidelined Dalton. With backup

CHAD OCHOCINCO

Chad Johnson's flashy receiving skills made him a Pro Bowler. His antics between plays turned even more heads, including those at the NFL office. The league regularly deemed his creative touchdown celebrations excessive, and he faced frequent fines for them. Yet perhaps his most surprising move came off the field. Johnson took on the nickname "Ochocinco," a play on the Spanish words for the numbers in his No. 85 jersey. In 2008, he legally changed his last name to Ochocinco so it would appear on the back of his jersey.

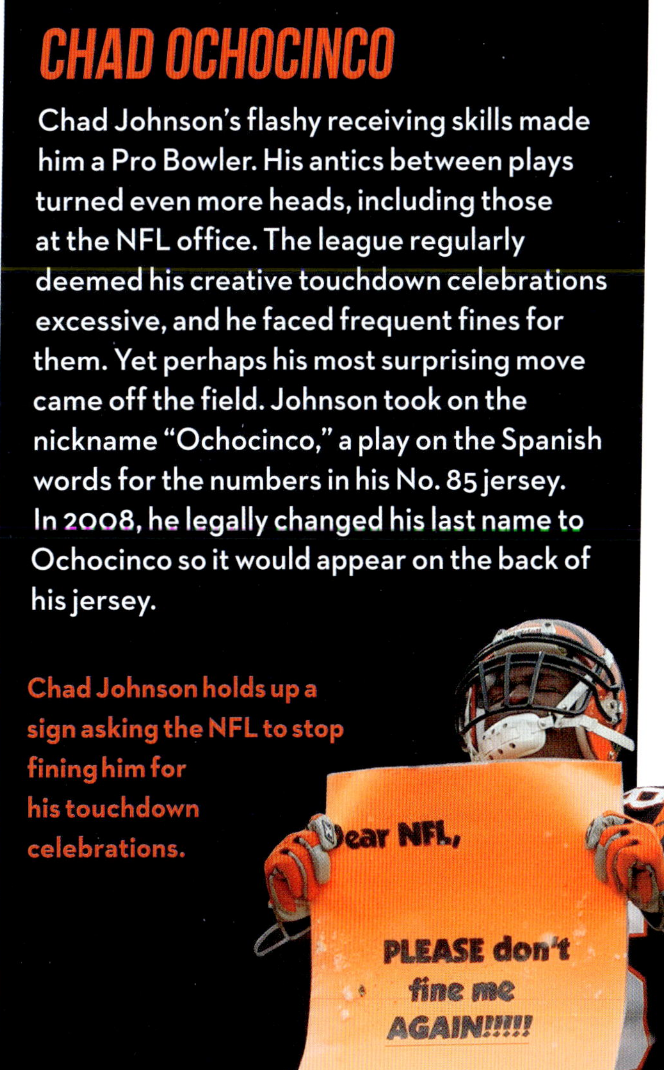

Chad Johnson holds up a sign asking the NFL to stop fining him for his touchdown celebrations.

quarterback A. J. McCarron starting in the playoffs, the Bengals fell to the Steelers 18–16.

Lewis had turned the Bengals back into a respectable team. By this point, though, Cincinnati fans were becoming frustrated with the playoff losses. Then the Bengals missed the playoffs altogether in 2016 and 2017. Despite fans' frustrations, Brown extended Lewis's contract. But when the Bengals finished 6–10 in 2018, even Brown had had enough. He fired Lewis after his 16th season as the Bengals head coach.

Joe Burrow threw for 2,688 yards and 13 touchdowns during his rookie season.

THE SAVIOR

The Bengals turned to Zac Taylor as their new head coach in 2019. And after the team struggled to a 2–14 record in his first season, the team turned to a new quarterback as well.

With the worst record in the league, the Bengals had the top pick in the 2020 draft. Experts agreed that LSU star quarterback Joe Burrow was the clear choice.

Burrow, who grew up in Ohio, appeared to be an obvious fit for the Bengals. However, some Burrow fans wanted him to refuse to play for the team. They didn't think he could succeed in Cincinnati, citing Brown's rocky record as owner. But Burrow was committed to turning the Bengals around, saying, "I'm going to work as hard as I can to bring winning to Cincinnati."

"I'M GOING TO WORK AS HARD AS I CAN TO BRING WINNING TO CINCINNATI."

—JOE BURROW

That didn't happen right away. While Burrow played well during his rookie year, he suffered a season-ending knee injury in Week 11. He recovered from the injury in time to start Week 1 of the 2021 season, and now he had his college teammate Ja'Marr Chase to throw to. NFL defenses struggled to contain the duo. With Burrow's strong arm and Chase's combination of size and speed, the two regularly connected on deep passes. Burrow set new team records with 4,611 passing yards and 34 touchdowns. Meanwhile, Chase easily won the NFL Offensive Rookie of the Year Award with 1,455 receiving yards and 13 touchdowns.

Behind the pair, the Bengals won 10 games to return to the playoffs for the first time since 2015. A record crowd of 66,277 fans packed Cincinnati's stadium when the Bengals faced the Las Vegas Raiders in the wild-card round. Chase racked up 116 receiving yards. But another rookie stepped up for the Bengals, too. Kicker Evan McPherson made all four of his field goal attempts to help lift the Bengals to their first playoff win in 31 years.

Bengals receiver Ja'Marr Chase catches a pass against the Las Vegas Raiders during their January 2022 playoff game.

The Bengals traveled to Tennessee to face the Titans in the next round. They left with an upset win thanks to McPherson's game-winning 52-yard field goal. That set up an AFC Championship Game against the Chiefs in Kansas City.

THRILLING REMATCH

Though the Bengals had beaten the Chiefs a few weeks earlier in the regular season to clinch the division title, few expected them to win the rematch on the road in the playoffs. After all, the Bengals were an inexperienced playoff team. The Chiefs had reached the previous two Super Bowls, winning one of them.

Cincinnati defenders sacked Kansas City Chiefs quarterback Patrick Mahomes (15) four times during the fourth quarter of the AFC Championship Game after the 2021 season.

The Chiefs showed their playoff savvy early. Superstar quarterback Patrick Mahomes ended the team's first three drives with touchdown passes to put the Chiefs ahead 21–3. But Burrow responded with a 41-yard touchdown pass to running back Samaje Perine on the next possession. Then the Bengals stopped the Chiefs at the goal line to keep the score 21–10 heading into halftime.

That stop provided a spark for the Bengals. They scored the next 14 points to take a 24–21 lead with 6:04 left in the game. However, as time expired, the Chiefs made a field goal to send the game to overtime.

The Chiefs had also gone to overtime in the previous round. In that game, they won the coin toss and quickly scored to secure the victory. The Chiefs tried to do that again after winning the coin toss against Cincinnati. Instead, Bengals safety Vonn Bell intercepted a deep pass by Mahomes. That meant the next score won. Cincinnati promptly ran eight plays to reach Kansas City's 13-yard line. From there, McPherson drilled an easy field goal to pull off a shocking win and send the Bengals on to Super Bowl LVI.

Bengals kicker Evan McPherson (2) celebrates his game-winning field goal in the AFC title game.

Facing the Los Angeles Rams in their home stadium, the Bengals got off to a slow start in the Super Bowl. Exciting young receiver Tee Higgins changed that. With the Bengals trailing 13–3 in the second

Bengals receiver Tee Higgins catches his first touchdown of Super Bowl LVI.

quarter, Burrow tossed the ball to running back Joe Mixon. When the defense keyed in on him, Mixon stepped back and launched a pass to Higgins, who was open in the end zone for a touchdown. On the first play of the second half, Higgins did it again. Shaking off his defender, Higgins grabbed a long pass from Burrow and took the ball 75 yards for a touchdown. Suddenly, the Bengals led 17–13.

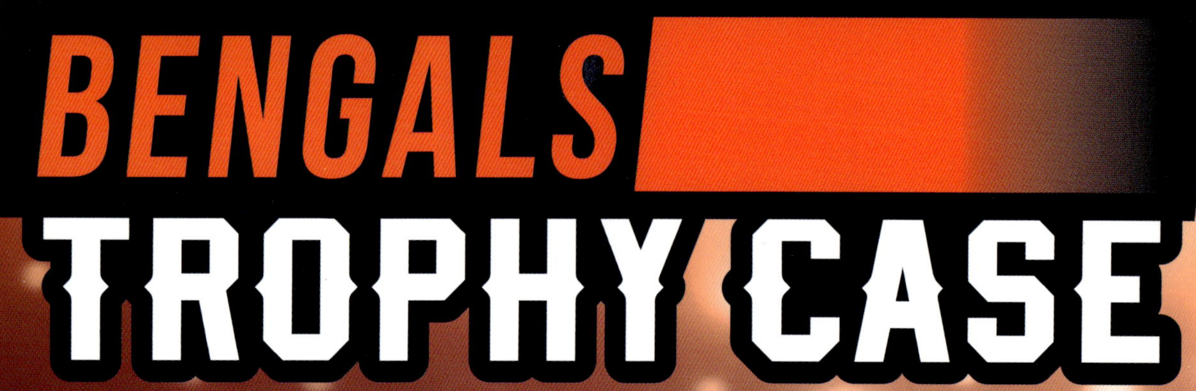

BENGALS TROPHY CASE

SUPER BOWL CHAMPIONSHIPS: 0

CONFERENCE CHAMPIONSHIPS: 3

1981, 1988, 2021

DIVISION TITLES: 12

AFC Central: 1970, 1973, 1981, 1982, 1988, 1990
AFC North: 2005, 2009, 2013, 2015, 2021, 2022

All stats are through the 2024 season.

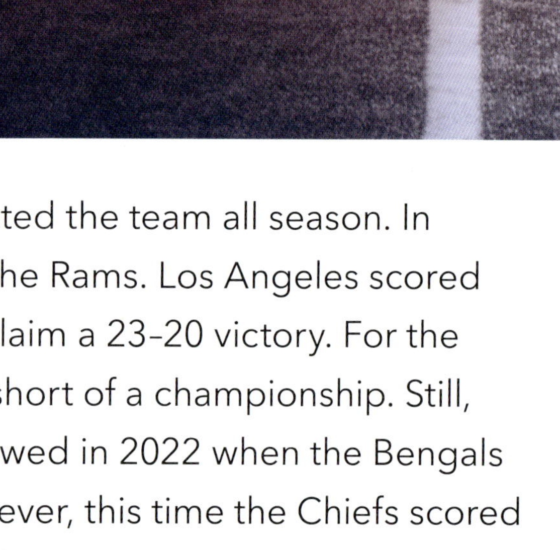

Cincinnati's star players had elevated the team all season. In the end, though, they couldn't stop the Rams. Los Angeles scored a late fourth-quarter touchdown to claim a 23–20 victory. For the third time, Cincinnati had fallen just short of a championship. Still, the future appeared bright. That showed in 2022 when the Bengals returned to the AFC title game. However, this time the Chiefs scored a last-second field goal as the Bengals once again lost 23-20.

With Burrow leading the way, the Bengals have shown they can compete with the NFL's best.

In Burrow, Chase, and Higgins, the Bengals boasted three of the NFL's most explosive offensive players. Returning to the top proved difficult, though. An injury kept Burrow out of the final seven games in 2023, and Cincinnati's nine wins weren't enough to make the playoffs. A five-game win streak to end the 2024 season got the Bengals back to 9–8, but once again, that record left them just shy of the playoffs. It was a disappointing finish for a team that wanted to be contending for championships, but with Burrow leading the way, fans hoped for better times ahead.

TIMELINE

The Bengals play in their first AFL season.

1968

1970

Following the AFL-NFL merger, the Bengals play in the NFL and become the fastest expansion team to make the playoffs.

After losing to the Oakland Raiders in the playoffs, Paul Brown steps down as Cincinnati's head coach.

1975

1982

Ken Anderson wins the NFL MVP Award and leads the Bengals to Super Bowl XVI on January 24.

Paul Brown hires Sam Wyche as the team's new head coach and drafts quarterback Boomer Esiason in the second round.

1984

1989

Thanks to an MVP season from Esiason, the Bengals make a run to Super Bowl XXIII on January 22.

Mike Brown takes over as Cincinnati's owner after his father, Paul Brown, dies.

1991

The Bengals draft A. J. Green and Andy Dalton and start a streak of five straight playoff appearances.

2011

The Bengals beat the Kansas City Chiefs in the AFC title game but then fall to the Los Angeles Rams in Super Bowl LVI on February 13.

2022

2003

In the same offseason, the Bengals hire Marvin Lewis and use the top pick in the draft on quarterback Carson Palmer.

2020

Cincinnati takes quarterback Joe Burrow with the first pick in the draft.

2023

The Bengals make it back to the AFC title game on January 29, but the Chiefs make a last-second field goal to win.

blitz—when a linebacker or defensive back attacks the line of scrimmage to stop a run or sack the quarterback.

commissioner—the chief executive of a sports league.

contract—an agreement to play for a certain team.

debut—first appearance.

draft—a system that allows teams to acquire new players coming into a league.

dynamic—energetic and exciting; in sports, usually referring to an athlete with one or more outstanding skills.

dynasty—a team that has an extended period of success, usually winning multiple championships in the process.

expansion team—a new team that is added to an existing league.

general manager—an executive who runs a team and is responsible for finding and signing players.

merge—join with another to create something new, such as a company, a team, or a league.

overtime—an extra period of play when the score is tied after regulation.

players' strike—when players refuse to work due to a disagreement between them and their employers (teams) about things such as working conditions or wages.

red zone—the area of the field between the 20-yard line and the goal line.

revolutionize—to change something in a significant way.

rookie—a professional athlete in his or her first year of competition.

route—a set path a receiver runs during a play to get open.

scheme—a set of formations that a team regularly uses.

scouting—looking for talented players.

upset—an unexpected victory by a supposedly weaker team or player.

veteran—someone who has played for many years.

wild-card—the first round of the playoffs.

ONLINE RESOURCES

To learn more about the Cincinnati Bengals, please visit **abdobooklinks.com** or scan this QR code. These links are routinely monitored and updated to provide the most current information available.

INDEX